The Canada Goose

NATURE WALK

NATURE WALK

The Canada Goose

James V. Bradley

CHELSEA CLUBHOUSE
An Imprint of Chelsea House Publishers

THE CANADA GOOSE

© 2006 by Infobase Publishing

Chelsea Clubhouse
An imprint of Infobase Publishing
132 West 31st Street
New York NY 10001

Library of Congress Cataloging-in-Publication Data

Bradley, James V. (James Vincent), 1931–
  The Canada goose / James V. Bradley.
     p. cm. — (Nature walk)
  Includes bibliographical references and index.
  ISBN 0-7910-9113-9 (hardcover)
  1. Canada goose—Juvenile literature. I. Title. II. Series: Bradley, James
V. (James Vincent), 1931– Nature walk.
  QL696.A52B72 2006
  598.4'178—dc22   2006011760

Chelsea House books are available at special discounts when purchased in bulk quantities for businesses, associations, institutions, or sales promotions. Please call our Special Sales Department in New York at (212) 967-8800 or (800) 322-8755.

You can find Chelsea House on the World Wide Web at
http://www.chelseahouse.com

TEXT AND COVER DESIGN by Takeshi Takahashi
ILLUSTRATIONS by William Bradley
SERIES EDITOR Tara Koellhoffer

Printed in the United States of America

BANG_PKG 10 9 8 7 6 5 4 3 2 1

This book is printed on acid-free paper.

All links and Web addresses were checked and verified to be correct at the time of publication. Because of the dynamic nature of the Web, some addresses and links may have changed since publication and may no longer be valid.

TABLE OF CONTENTS

Chapter 1

Introduction to the Canada Goose

IN 1758, SWEDISH BOTANIST Carolus Linnaeus published a book that gave animals and plants Latin names. Among them was a bird named *Branta canadensis interior*, which we know today as one race of the Canada goose. Linnaeus did more than just name animals and plants. He established a system of classification that later drew attention to the idea that some animals seem to be related to one another. Is a goose more closely related to a chicken or a squirrel? We know

The Canada goose is known as *Branta canadensis* under
Carolus Linnaeus's system of animal classification.

now that the goose and chicken have a more recent common ancestor than the goose and squirrel. It was not so obvious in 1758.

Distribution of Races of Canada Geese

Different races of Canada geese keep their nesting sites in certain general locations. New generations

---

THE CANADA GOOSE

Scientific Name: *Branta canadensis interior**
(Genus) (Species) (Race)

Genus *Branta:* A large group of geese that includes the Canada goose, barnacle goose, and brant.

Species *canadensis:* All Canada geese belong to the same species. All have a black head and neck, a conspicuous white patch on the cheek, black legs and feet, and a white V-shaped band at the base of the tail. Members of the same species can mate and produce fertile offspring.

Race *interior:* *Race* is another term meaning "subspecies" or "variety." Members of a particular race differ from other races in superficial ways, such as size, markings, and the paths they travel for migration, or movement through different seasons. Isolation of races usually prevents mating between races. Some scientists believe there are 10 to 12 different races of Canada geese.

*There are many races of Canada goose, but *Branta canadensis interior* is one of the most common. It is used here as an example.

return each spring and vigorously defend their home sites. Different nesting sites have different environments, and geese go through physical changes to suit their environment. When a population becomes so distinct that it can be distinguished from other populations, scientists label it as a new race.

How Might Geese Change Over Time?

Imagine a small population of dark-colored geese nesting in a region of light-colored grasses. Over a period of years, **gene mutations** may introduce new traits, such as buff-colored feathers, into the population. Geese with these new light-colored feathers blend in better with the light-colored grasses. Predators such as coyotes and raccoons that like to eat eggs are more likely to spot dark-colored geese, which makes their nests more vulnerable to attacks. Because the change in feather color protects the geese that have lighter-colored feathers, over time, more light-colored geese survive to breed than dark-colored geese, and the population changes, or shifts, to a light color. The light color is an environmental **adaptation** that results from the forces of **natural selection**.

With the passage of time, a population may change so much that it can no longer reproduce with other races of Canada geese. It then becomes a new species.

Adaptations

Adaptations are the result of environmental forces in nature that change a species over time. All Canada geese have a few adaptations in common.

All Canada geese have black necks and heads with white cheek patches that help break up the outline of

The traits that help geese survive in their environment will be passed down to their offspring. That fact is the basis for the theory of natural selection.

CANADA GOOSE FACTS

Height: 20–48"
Weight: 3–24 pounds
Life Span:
  Average: 10–25 years
  Maximum: 42 (in captivity)
Flight Speed: 10–50 mph
Range: All of the United States, lower portions of each Canadian province, northern Mexico
Habitats: Wetlands, marshes, lakes, streams, rivers, coastal areas, urban retention/detention basins
Foods: Grains, succulents, grasses, pondweeds, lawns in urban areas

the bird. This serves a function similar to that of zebra stripes, providing camouflage for the animal to help it hide from predators.

The Canada goose's bones are thin and hollow to reduce weight for flight. The legs and feet are black and covered with scales, a feature that remains from the goose's past as a reptile. (Millions of years ago, before birds **evolved**, the ancestors of modern birds were reptiles.) In the winter, increased blood supply can warm the feet and the black color absorbs heat. In the summer, when it flies, the goose can spread its webbed feet and cool its blood.

Size is also an adaptation: Small geese migrate greater distances. If migration routes get longer, the average size of a goose population will get smaller over time.

The goose is not equipped to swim under water to look for food, but its snake-like neck lets it reach

The Canada goose cannot swim under water, but it can reach its long neck beneath the water to look for food.

under the water to grab aquatic plants, seeds, and bulbs. The length of the goose's neck is another characteristic that varies with race.

Scientists once thought feathers were modified from the scales seen on the reptilian ancestors of birds. Recent studies of how feathers develop, however, show that feathers evolved on reptiles independently from scales. Today, feathers are found only on birds. Without feathers, there could be no flight. Besides flight feathers on the wings, a goose has contour feathers that shape the body and down feathers that keep it warm.

Adaptation to Life in the Air

The word *Archaeopteryx* means "ancient wing"—an appropriate name for an early prehistoric bird that is the oldest bird known to science. The first *Archaeopteryx* fossil, a single feather, was discovered in Germany in 1860. Since then, eight more *Archaeopteryx* fossils have been found.

Archaeopteryx was basically a cross between a bird and a dinosaur. It lived 150 million years ago, during the Jurassic Period. It had feathers and hollow bones like the birds we know today. However, it also had traits in common with dinosaurs, including teeth and a long, bony tail. It could walk on two legs and was a predator that ate meat, had four wings, and glided between the trees.

CHINA'S FEATHERED DINOSAURS

Fossils found in China in 2003 helped scientists understand how feathers and flight developed. Feather development follows a sequence, with each type of feather replacing the type that came before it. Some of the feathered dinosaurs had only pin feathers, which are small tubes that stick out of the skin. In other dinosaurs, pin feathers gave rise to fluffy down feathers, which are good for keeping the body warm. Still other feathered dinosaurs had both down and contour, or body, feathers. From these, flight feathers later developed in modern birds.

The four-winged dinosaur (*Microraptor gui*) shown below had all four types of feathers. This dinosaur climbed trees to gain height and then leaped off to glide to another tree.

The Canada goose we know today has descended from dinosaurs that went extinct millions of years ago.

The next time you see a flock of Canada geese grazing on a lawn with their scaled legs and snake-like necks, think of dinosaurs. These birds—and all others, from sparrow to ostrich—are the surviving relatives of the dinosaurs that became extinct over 60 million years ago.

Chapter 2

Migration and Lifestyle

How Geese Migrate

Migrating geese were a source of food for the North American Indians before European settlers arrived on the continent. Sometimes the geese appear as tiny specks in the sky, flying as high as 9,000 feet (2,743 m) and at speeds of 70 miles (113 km) per hour. They use the position of the sun and stars and undoubtedly things we are unaware of to guide them as they fly. During their flight, they memorize the physical features of the land. Along the **Mississippi flyway**, for example, the Canada geese commit to memory the tributaries of the river, sandbars, swamps, and natural pools where they rest and feed. Over the past 200 years, levees and other deep-water navigation features have destroyed much of the Mississippi River's natural habitats, but geese have adapted to be able to survive in the new terrain.

The cities of Chicago and Milwaukee were once wetlands that contained food for many different species of waterfowl. These were also favorite hunting

The Canada goose migrates great distances with the changing of the seasons.

grounds for Indians. Now that these wetlands have dried up, they have been replaced by wetlands such as Nacedah in Wisconsin, Crab Orchard in Illinois, and other refuges developed by federal and state fish and wildlife departments as well as environmental groups. The conversion of prairies to farms and the growth of cities have been major factors in increasing geese populations. Grain left behind after the harvesting of wheat and corn as well as acres of tender new grass shoots have greatly increased the migrating geese's strength and reproductive success.

Why Do Geese Migrate?

The urge to migrate is a natural response to changes in the environment. Changes in temperature and the length of daylight are two of the known factors that trigger this response.

Another is **reproduction**. Unlike humans, Canada geese reproduce at only one time of year. The geese's spring migration to their northern breeding grounds keeps pace with the beginning of warmer weather. It starts as the more southern states reach temperatures of about 35°F (1.7°C), usually in early February. As temperatures get warmer farther north, the geese follow. By the end of April, the geese's northernmost nesting sites in Canada are usually occupied, even though the snow and ice have not completely melted yet. If necessary, the geese can live off their own body fat until mid-May, when the breeding grounds offer ideal conditions. These include good nesting close to water, plenty of plants and insects to eat, and few predators to bother the geese.

Two Common Races in the Midwest

The expansion of the Canada goose is remarkable, considering that the *Branta canadensis maxima* race of Canada goose was reported to be extinct as recently as 1962. Much of the expansion of the

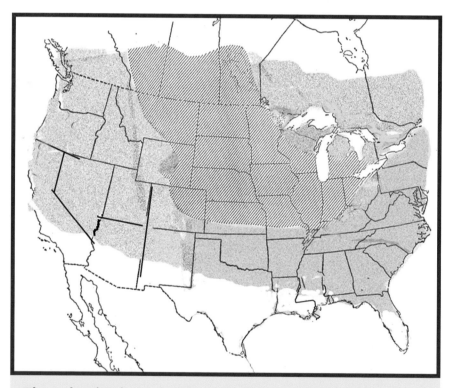

The red striped area is where the largest Canada geese, *Branta canadensis maxima*, nested before Europeans came to North America. The blue shaded portion of the map shows the areas to which these geese have expanded since then.

geese's territory occurred in the last 40 years. As their numbers increased, they invaded new territories and were exported to other states where people were interested in hunting. These birds are sometimes called "resident geese" since many stay in one place year-round. Their numbers are now so great that they are considered pests in many areas. In some places, they compete with migrating geese for limited food and nesting sites.

The *Branta canadensis interior* race of Canada goose winters at the Mississippi–Ohio river junction. Its migration involves a 1,300-mile (2,092-km) trip along the Mississippi flyway to and from nesting grounds along the southwestern shores of Hudson Bay. The geese migrate along **corridors**—paths— within the flyway, stopping to rest and feed at the Horicon National Wildlife Refuge near Mayville, Wisconsin. During their fall migration, the number of geese at Horicon can reach 150,000.

Migration Behaviors

When you think of the term *migration*, the image of geese in a V-formation may immediately come to mind. The geese that fly in a V-formation are often members of an extended family that raise their young in the same nesting grounds.

The V-formation is an energy-saving method that has its basis in the physics of moving an object through the water or air. When you row a boat, turbulence occurs in the water in the form of small swirls, similar to water going down a drain, with each completed stroke of your oar. A plane in flight creates a similar effect. A circular swirl of air forms at the tip of each wing. Air flows downward behind each wingtip and upward out from the wingtip. The result is a spiral of air that trails behind each wing. The swirling air currents are so strong that they can cause a plane that follows another plane too closely to crash.

Canada geese fly their migration routes in the typical V-formation, seen here.

Animal ecologists Malte Andersson and Johan Wallander reported that the same properties of physics apply to the flight of large birds. A V is formed when each goose in line moves slightly outward to gain lift from the upward movement of air created by the goose in front of it. In addition to saving energy, each goose gets a clear view forward, which decreases the chance of a collision, and a clear view of the ground so they can view the route. If a goose moves out of line, it instantly feels the loss of lift and moves back into position. The geese's constant honking communicates to all the birds how well the flight is going and reinforces bonding within the group.

The lead goose uses more energy than the others. When it gets tired, it drops back and another adult takes its place at the front of the V-formation.

According to Andersson and Wallander, V-formations are maintained by parental concern for

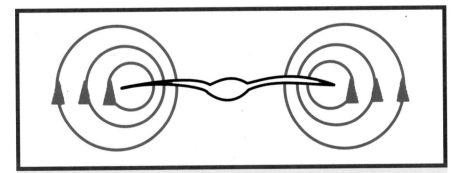

When a goose flaps its wings, swirls of air form at the tip of each wing.

HITCHING A RIDE NORTH?

There have been sporadic reports of small birds such as hummingbirds and wrens being found embedded in the feathers of geese that were making their northern migration. It is believed that these birds were hitching a ride north. This does make sense. Think of the energy these birds would save! Supposedly, what the small birds do is burrow into the soft feathers on the back of a goose and stay there for the journey north. If you've ever seen your fingers almost disappear into the dense feathers of a goose, you can understand that this would be an ideal way for a small bird to make a long journey.

their young. V-formations allow young geese, especially those that are making their first long migration, to keep up with the adults. The younger, weaker geese take the positions that require them to use the least energy.

When large numbers of unrelated geese fly together, however, the pattern of flight is often bow-like. With this bow pattern, the energy created by flight is more fairly distributed among individuals; each goose gains a partial lift from its neighbor. As you watch this formation, you will often see it break up and reform. Some breakups happen because of wind or when individual geese get tired and drop back. Sometimes family members leave the bow to form their own group in the more familiar V-formation.

Different flocks of migrating geese confine themselves to loosely defined corridors. In this way, there is less stress on feeding areas within different corridors. The expansion of city areas and the drainage of wetlands within a corridor can make the flight time between food and rest stops longer and make migration more difficult. This problem has greatly reduced the populations of migrating waterfowl in California. In the fall and winter months, geese head for areas that offer food, water, and protection from predators.

Migrating geese tend to fly along familiar routes, known as corridors.

Hunting

Thousands of migrating geese are killed each season. Hunters claim that the practice helps control the goose population, but geese are smart and they learn fast. It takes only one hunting experience to see how very crafty they are. One shiny gun barrel poking out of a blind, a bright button, or any movement is enough to alert the lead goose to fly away from hunters. Organizations that oppose hunting claim that hunting does not have an effect on managing geese populations and that the killing and maiming of these birds should be stopped.

Chapter 3

Where and How Geese Live

Permanent Resident Geese

Resident geese are those birds that don't migrate. They stay in the same general area all year-round because they have food sources available. The typical "pest" geese are the ones that have their nesting sites in or near suburban areas, especially in the Atlantic and midwestern states. In Minnesota, for instance, warm water from a power plant in Rochester as well as sources of food from nearby farms and friendly people provide ideal conditions year-round for the area's resident geese.

Many people think of the Canada goose as a pest animal, since the birds often stay on lawns and golf courses all year-round.

The overwhelming majority of resident geese are *Branta canadensis maxima*, the giant Canada goose. They are found in varying numbers in all states. About one-third of all geese that occupy the Atlantic flyway, which stretches from Florida to Ontario, are giants. The giants do migrate to their place of birth, but this may be a relatively short distance. Some Illinois giants migrate to nesting sites within the state, while others migrate to Illinois from nearby Wisconsin and Indiana, and some from as far away as Mississippi.

Some migrating geese join the resident geese in urban and suburban areas as a way to avoid hunters. They are actually landing right in the "enemy camp."

WHAT ARE RESIDENT GEESE?

When geese have been hatched and reared in the suburbs, they lack the experience of migrating to their historical nesting sites. When they are ready to reproduce, these geese simply return to their suburban nesting sites. Because they stay in the same general area all the time, never making long migrations, they are called "resident" geese.

Estimates show that giant Canada geese (*Branta canadensis maxima*) are approaching 50% of the total number of all resident geese, and they are the ones that cause most of the problems related to geese as pest animals.

Canada geese need to live in areas that offer access to plenty of water. If not enough water is available, the area will no longer be an attractive home for geese.

Canada geese are grazers, and they love tender grass shoots. In fact, an ideal habitat that can feed large populations of geese and also meet all of their other needs is a golf course. The best way to discourage geese from inhabiting golf courses is to decrease the number of water hazards on the course, which takes away easy access to water.

Problems with Resident Geese

In suburban North America, the biggest problem with geese is that the tender grass shoots they eat pass through their digestive systems only partly digested. A giant Canada goose can produce one pound (0.45 kg) of waste each day. Most complaints about the goose problem come from specific areas where their droppings destroy lawns, make walking in those areas unpleasant, and contaminate beaches and reservoirs with bacteria. Some farmers complain of crop loss, although others appreciate the fact that the geese clean up last year's kernels from the cornfields.

A typical cry of frustration against the Canada goose is: "Go back where you came from!" The trouble is, Canada geese were in North America before the Europeans settled here. With their farms, then with towns, and finally with cities and highways, the people destroyed native geese habitats. Prairie grasses were replaced by corn, wheat, and suburban lawns. Such destruction of habitats can eliminate many species, and it has harmed many animals, but not the geese. The native grasses were replaced by non-native turf grass, an ideal goose food. Abundant food throughout the United States was the main reason for the population explosion and the territorial expansion of the giant Canada geese.

Large numbers of Canada geese can often be found in suburban parks, golf courses, and corporate lawns.

Solutions to the Goose Problem

Many methods of reducing the goose population have been tried. Some are controversial and some are expensive, but all are partially successful, and most have drawbacks.

Border collies can be trained to chase geese from golf courses, reservoirs, and parks. Geese do not like areas where visibility is poor, so cattails and brush can be grown around ponds. A hunting season for resident geese in safe areas can be initiated. People can stop feeding geese. Shooting blanks can discourage geese from nesting. Corporate landscapes can be redesigned to replace ponds with fountains and to decorate the lawns with sculpture. The number of ponds on golf courses can be reduced. Experiments with using lasers to haze geese have had some limited success. More research looking into methods of goose birth control may also be supported by state and federal governments.

When people demand that the number of geese be drastically reduced, what they really want is for geese to be removed from areas where they cause problems.

Some communities in Michigan, New York, and Minnesota have resorted to killing adult geese and goslings by rounding them up during the **molting season** when they cannot fly. The geese are sent to food-processing plants, and their meat is distributed to the poor. In some past cases, meat processed from

Not feeding geese is one way to make suburban areas less attractive to these birds.

these geese was found to be unsafe to eat because of the accumulation of poisons from herbicides and pesticides used on lawns and farmlands. This solution is only temporary because more geese will eventually move into a good feeding or nesting area.

Chapter 4

Goose Family Life

Courtship

Geese usually reproduce by the time they reach the age of three. They mate for life (which may last 20 or more years), but if one member of a goose couple dies, the other may take a new mate within a year or two.

Mating takes place on water. Usually, both birds start by dipping their heads under water, then lifting them up to throw water over their backs. The male may proceed with a courting ritual called the "triumph ceremony," where he attacks an imaginary enemy. The ceremony

In a triumph ceremony, a male goose (left) courts a female (right) by chasing an imaginary rival (bottom right).

begins when the male swims toward the female and seems to concentrate on an imagined rival off to her side. With his mouth open, tongue protruding, neck stretched out, and head lowered, he attacks. As he beats his wings, he plunges forward, splashing water. The "attack" is accompanied by a raucous cackling while the female watches.

If the female is impressed by the male's display, she responds by coming forward to meet him. She hisses and fluffs her feathers, lowering her head in submission. In return, the male gives a triumphant cackle. He then passes his neck around hers and swims alongside her. While holding her neck gently in his beak, he climbs onto her back in order to mate.

Geese mate for life. Only if the original partner dies will a goose look for a new mate.

After mating, both geese may dip their heads and throw water over their backs, and then stretch their necks high, with heads and beaks lifted. A good sign of bonding is when the female joins the male in fighting off rivals from her chosen nesting site.

A wide range of variations of this courting ritual can be seen throughout the year, and portions of it are even performed by young geese. Parts of this mating ritual can be observed between mated geese in everyday life. This behavior serves to reinforce bonding, especially if the geese have been separated for a time, just like hugging and kissing in humans.

Nesting

The female chooses a nesting site, and some geese pairs have been known to return to the same site for seven consecutive years. The female scrapes out a slight depression with her body. She sits in this hole and gathers sticks, dry grass, moss, and aquatic

The female goose lays about three to eight eggs in a nest she has built.

vegetation from the surrounding area. Both the male and female defend the nest.

Sometimes, young geese will fly off to stay on open water. If space and food are plentiful, however, they and other close kin may stay around and help raise the young. Yet if youngsters from last year's family hang around too long, they are chased away.

Usually, a female goose lays a **clutch** of three to eight eggs. She plucks **down** from her breast to protect the eggs from extreme heat and cold. Only the female sits on the nest, while the male stands guard. Each time the female leaves and returns, she covers the eggs with more down to protect them. Predators are always waiting for a chance to snatch an unguarded egg.

Incubation lasts about 29 days, and many things can go wrong. Cold weather, hailstorms, or a sudden downpour are among the natural hazards that threaten a goose nest. If the eggs get too cold, the unhatched goslings inside them will die. Speedboats that make waves can also wipe out goose nests.

An overpopulation of nesting snow geese in the coastal tundra around Hudson Bay in northern Canada is currently destroying the geese's feeding grounds, and the destruction is spreading to the nesting sites of Canada geese. A loss of good nesting sites can cause a decrease in the number of successful hatchings. Under such conditions, Canada geese have been known to abandon their eggs.

Growing Up as a Goose

The shelled egg first appeared in reptiles. Unlike the amphibian egg, which had to be laid in water, the shelled egg had its own water and food supply. This allowed reptiles to move onto the land. Birds inherited their egg-laying ability from certain ancestral reptiles.

A Canada goose egg is about 2.5 to 3 inches (6.4 to 7.6 cm) long. Its shell is made of protein, calcium carbonate, and other minerals, making it strong enough to support the weight of the parent and yet porous enough for gases to pass through while keeping out dangerous bacteria. Chicks make a peeping sound even before they break out of the shell.

Goslings weigh about 2 ounces (57 g) when they hatch and are covered with down. In chilly weather, the goslings can fluff up their down feathers, increasing the amount of trapped air and improving the insulation. They can see at birth and are able to walk and even feed themselves by picking at plants and insects.

Goslings have an egg tooth on the tip of their beaks, which they use to make the first break in the shell when they hatch. This tooth drops off or wears away soon after hatching.

After an incubation period of about 29 days, all of the eggs hatch within a 24-hour period. The goslings leave the nest within the next 24 hours. Their parents then lead them to the water, with one parent leading and one bringing up the rear.

A gosling uses the egg tooth on the tip of its beak to help it break out of its egg.

Goose parents lead goslings to water within 24 hours after they hatch.

As more clutches hatch, groups join together to form large **creches**, which are essentially goose day-care nurseries. The guardians of a creche may be other goose pairs, aunts and uncles, or non-breeding siblings. This system frees the parents to look for food after a long period of guarding the nest. The goslings of different parents accept one another and other adults as part of their family. In a matter of weeks, the goslings become more independent of their parents.

Both parents stay with their goslings to keep them safe.

Swimming goslings are a prime target for a variety of predators that attack both from above and below water. They are threatened from below by pike, muskellunge, snapping turtles, and other creatures. Geese have little defense against these predators, but a creche increases the chances for individual survival. Heading into brush or reeds also offers protection.

It takes about 70 days from the time they hatch before goslings make their first flight, and this is a dangerous time for young geese. Adults go through a molt at this time that takes about 40 days. They cannot

THE WILD GOOSE DECATHLON OF HERMANN, MISSOURI

The *Branta canadensis maxima* goslings of Hermann, Missouri, face a tough upbringing. They must survive a high dive within 24 hours after they hatch. Here's how it happens:

Nesting sites are located on limestone cliffs 150 to 200 feet above the nearby Missouri River. Goslings hatch in late April, and within 24 hours of their birth, adult geese encourage them to jump over the cliff. The light, fluffy goslings, which weigh only 3 ounces, can survive a lot of bumps on the way down, but some don't make it.

Still, the survival of most of the goslings ensures the continued use of this unusual nesting site. The cliffs dramatically reduce the loss of goslings to predators. A fox trying to raid a nest could easily be pushed off the cliff by an angry goose parent.

fly when they are molting, so they are vulnerable to predators. Adults are especially nervous during this time and will show aggressive behavior if they feel threatened or if their young are approached.

Imprinting

How do goslings know to follow their parents? This question was answered when scientists discovered that goslings will follow the first moving object they see after they hatch. This process is

Groups of adults and young, called creches, help keep goslings safe from predators.

called **imprinting**, and it explains why goslings will follow their parents to open water within 24 hours after hatching. If the first moving object they see is a human, however, the human becomes the parent, and the goslings will follow the human. Imprinting is an important evolutionary survival mechanism in many animals, especially mammals.

In the 1930s, Austrian behavioral biologist Konrad Lorenz first used the term *imprinting*. Although he did his work with Greylag geese, Canada geese obey the same natural laws. Imprinting also became a

Goslings will follow the first moving object they see after hatching. This process is called "imprinting."

Because of imprinting, goslings will usually follow an adult goose. If the first moving object they see is a human, however, the human becomes the parent, and the young geese will follow the human.

dominant idea in early investigations of how human babies bond with their mothers.

Bill Lishman, a Toronto sculptor and a flyer of ultralight aircraft, fulfilled a boyhood desire to fly with birds. He knew about imprinting and performed a remarkable experiment. He played a recording of the sound of his ultralight aircraft both before and after his goslings hatched so that the goslings associated the sound of the motor with their parent. Then by being present when goslings hatched, he became the "father" of a flock of goslings and set out to lead them on a new migration route. The goslings accepted Lishman as their parent and followed him as he flew his aircraft.

In Lishman's book, *Father Goose*, he describes how on October 19, 1994, after some practice flights, he and his 18 "offspring" took off in a V-formation and started their 36-mile (58-km) flight across Lake Ontario. They headed for the Airlie Federal Refuge in Virginia. With several stops along the way, they made the 350-mile (563-km) trip safely. In the later northern migration, from Virginia back to Ontario, 16 of the 18 geese returned.

Chapter 5

Goose Behavior

Goose Body Language
Human-like traits such as aggression, submission, anxiety, and fear are expressed by a goose's body language and in the sounds it makes. If people watch closely, they can easily understand how a goose feels.

When a Goose Gets Nervous
Children are often attracted to geese, especially when the geese have young goslings. However, this is when the adult geese are most aggressive. When adults feel

When feeding geese, people must be sure to remain calm so the geese don't feel threatened.

threatened, they act nervous and move toward the threat. They may pump their heads up and down, or show other signs of anxiety. As their anxiety grows, geese approach with their heads low and necks bent back. They may hiss. This is when the bird's reptilian ancestry is most evident. Usually, this warning is enough to encourage people to back off. But if a goose extends its neck with its head low, it may nip, usually at the person's legs. If the goose feels severely threatened, the nip may be very painful, since its beak is lined with a row of small but sharp saw-like teeth.

In fighting for its life, a goose can deliver powerful blows with its wings. It is hard to believe, but geese, especially *Branta canadensis maxima*, can hit with such force that they can break a grown man's arm.

Watch a group of geese feeding and find the sentinel. The sentinel is the goose that appears to be alert and watchful. It will be standing still or moving slowly, slightly sideways to people who approach it. With its neck straight and head horizontal, the sentinel studies anything or anyone who seems threatening.

Another, less aggressive goose response to a threatening situation is to hold its head high and

DID YOU KNOW?

Canada Goose Identification Tips:
- Length: 16–25 inches
- Wingspan: 50–68 inches
- Sexes look similar
- Large long-necked goose
- Black bill
- Black head and neck
- White throat patch extends up to cheek
- Brown back, upper wing and flanks
- Brownish-white breast and belly
- White upper tail feathers contrast with black tail
- White undertail feathers
- Great size variation, with some northern subspecies duck-sized

In a group of geese, the sentinel always watches for danger.

move it up and down rapidly. This is a sign that the bird is unsure of the situation and feels threatened.

When a goose's neck is extended up and the head rapidly turns from side to side, the bird is annoyed at something and feels some mild stress. It may, for example, be trying to influence others to fly to another feeding area.

When a goose's head and bill are pointed down toward its breast, the bird is showing submission or inferior status. When the neck is first drawn back and then partially extended, this represents a response to a mild threat to the goose's territory. This sometimes happens when someone is feeding geese and one goose intrudes on another's space. If the goose's anxiety increases, the goose will extend its neck low and horizontal to the ground, with its mouth opened, and do some hissing. The next act is to rush and nip the intruding goose, but usually, the only damage that results is the loss of a few tail feathers.

Goose Acrobatics

A goose's behavior can also be funny to see. When geese land in fields or on small ponds, especially in heavy winds, they honk to announce their arrival, and then they perform some fabulous acrobatics. In order to lose altitude rapidly because of the wind, they partially close one wing. This causes them to tip to one side and fall or slide down at an angle. They

Geese are always alert to sounds made around them.

Geese can perform some amazing acrobatics, especially when they land in water or fields.

spread both wings again to gain some control and then fold the opposite wing. Sometimes this makes them tip as much as 90 degrees, but some observers have reported seeing a complete somersault. The typical result is a controlled zigzag fall that usually ends with a perfect landing.

adaptation—Making changes, either physically or in behavior, to better survive in the environment.

carnivorous—Meat-eating.

clutch—Term used for a group of goose eggs.

corridors—Migration routes.

creches—Groups of young geese watched over by adults.

down—Soft, fluffy feathers that help keep the body warm.

evolved—Changed over time to better survive in the environment.

gene mutation—A change in the genetic makeup of a living thing.

imprinting—The process in which newly hatched goslings follow the first moving object they see. Usually, this is the parent goose, but it can be a human.

Mississippi flyway—The route from the Arctic coastal plain in Canada, over the Great Lakes, and down to the Mississippi River delta.

molting season—The period, usually from early June to late July, when geese lose their wing feathers and are unable to fly.

natural selection—The theory that says that those animals with traits that help them adapt better to their
environment than others will survive to reproduce,
creating more animals with the same traits.

reproduction—The process of mating and
creating offspring.

Breen, Kit Howard. *Canada Goose*. Stillwater, MN: Voyageur Press, 1990.

Brush, A. H. "On the Origin of Feathers." *Journal of Evolutionary Biology 9* (1996): 131–142.

Gee, H. "Fossil Boosts Trees-down Start for Flight." *Nature Science Update; Perspective on Ref 1.* January 23, 2003.

Lishman, Bill. *Father Goose and His Goslings*. Seattle: Storytellers, Inc., 1992.

Web Sites

General information
http://www.canadageese.com

International Goose Research Group
http://www.goose.org

National Geographic
http://news.nationalgeographic.com/news/2003/01/0121_030122_dromaeosaur.html

BIBLIOGRAPHY

"Aircraft to Play Mother Goose in Unusual Rescue Experiment," *The New York Times*, August 30, 1994.

Andersson, Malte, and Johan Wallander. "Kin Selection and Reciprocity in Flight Formation?" *Behavioral Ecology* 15(1) (2004): 153–162.

Chew, Ryan. "Stakeout: A Tale of Two Species." *Chicago Wilderness Magazine*, Fall 2005.

Lishman, Bill. *Father Goose*. New York: Crown Publishers, 1996.

Mississippi Flyway Council. "Distribution Map of Races: Composite of Information From Management Plan for the Mississippi Valley Population of Canada Geese." July 1997–2002.

Seideman, D. "Earning Their Wings the Hard Way." *National Wildlife* 23 (1985): 42–45.

Sherman, D. E., and A. E. Barras. "Efficacy of a Laser Device for Hazing Canada Geese from Urban Areas of Northeast Ohio." *Ohio Journal of Science* 103 (3) (2004): 38–42.

Wilford, John Nobile. "Fossil of 4-Winged Dinosaur Casts Light on Birds and Flight," *The New York Times*, January 23, 2003.

Xing Xu et al. "Four-winged Dinosaurs From China." *Nature* 421 (2003). Available online at *http://www.amonline.net.au/chinese_dinosaurs/ feathered_dinosaurs/ photo_gallery.htm.*

PICTURE CREDITS

ABOUT THE AUTHOR

James V. Bradley, coauthor of *Modern Biology*, taught biology at Lake Forest High School in Lake Forest, Illinois, for 25 years. He also taught science in Colorado and in the United Kingdom. Bradley received the Illinois STAR Award (Science Teaching Achievement Recognition) in 1980 and was named by the National Association of Biology Teachers as outstanding biology teacher in Illinois in 1981. He retired from teaching in 1994, but continues to write and study science topics.